JE SUIS CHARLIE

Tyler Stowe

ISBN-13: 978-1507546215
ISBN-10: 1507546211

Library of Congress Control cataloging -publication data.

Published in the United States of America 2014.

Printed in the United States of America.

First Edition

A blind leads
A blind and they
both fall into the
ditch.

JE SUIS

CHARLIE

Tyler Stowe

TABLE OF CONTENT

PRELIMINARY

Charlie Hebdo is a French satirical weekly newspaper, featuring cartoons, reports, polemics, and jokes. Impertinent and forcefully in tone, a publication describes as anti-racist, publishing articles on the extreme right, religion (Catholicism, Islam, Judaism), politics, culture. According to its former editor Stephan Charbonnier, the magazine's editorial viewpoint reflects "all components of left wing pluralism."

Charlie Hebdo first appeared in 1970 as a successor to the Hara-Kiri magazine, which was banned for mocking the death of former French President Charles De Gaulle. In 1981 publication ceased, but the magazine was resurrected in 1992. The magazine's current editor is Gerard Biard who took over the role when Charbonnier, who had been editor since 2009, was killed. The previous editors were François Cavanna and Philippe Val. The magazine is published every Wednesday, with special editions issued on an unscheduled basis.

The magazine has been the target of two terrorist attacks, in 2011 alleged to be in response to a number of controversial Muhammad cartoons it published.

On Wednesday they became the most wanted terrorists in France after they shot to death 10 journalists, two Police Officers at the headquarters of the satirical magazine Charlie Hebdo. They also murdered 5 more

Jewish customers at a Kosher Market and a printing factory as they tried to escape later on.

"A picture is worth a thousand words." It turns out that one cartoon worth thousand articles. The cartoon's strength is that it's required only brief attention. Therefore, it represents the ultimate freedom of speech, direct and clear. Freedom of expression is the only tool, of freedom of thought. The worldwide media need to channel all the newspapers and TV networks and publish the cartoon which took the Islamic killers crazy. It should be posted it on the first page, in the center, and in large print, on all languages, continents and countries.

It's not a sufficient response to the terrible massacre in Paris, but it's a first proper response.

Said and Shérif Kouachi resided in the 19th district of Paris. They used to pray in the mosque located near the Stalingrad metro station. The 19th district is in the north of the French capital. This is a popular district that many inhabitants are immigrants and foreigners, North Africans, Jews, Pakistanis, Vietnamese and Chinese. In the past three years there have been several shooting incidents against Jewish buildings. Some of them were directed at the local synagogue and other at two stores belonging to Jews. All have ended without casualties. A few steps away, there is a large butcher shop where signs are posted in French and Arabic.

Élan is an Israeli who owns a store in that street. He is selling jeans on that street, and he claimed that Said Kouachi was generally a nice person, but he believed that Kouachi used drugs. He believed that the two brothers were on the street just because people knew them and they didn't try to hide.

"Said Kouachi the older brother, he used to hang around here with his friends, and everyone knew him in the street."

"Did you recognize him when he came out of the car?"

"Of course. I think he also recognized me."

"He could kill you!?"

"He could, but he did not hurt me. He was my client and often came to buys jeans from me. I do not think he wanted to kill Jews."

"They wanted everyone to know that what he is doing. Said Kouachi had left his ID in the car on purpose, so they would know it was him who did the killing and will talk about it. I think they were trying to impress the young Muslim community here. There will be young Muslims here who wish to do similar things."

"What was he wearing?"

"Usually he wore jeans and sometimes had a Galabiya on his head. He did not always have a beard."

"Why do you think he decided to commit murder like this?"

"I guess he has been brainwashed."

M, the owner of three large kosher bakeries in the district, said that the nature of his relationship with Muslims is 'Okay.'

"You can ask my neighbor, he's a Muslim, and own a nearby grocery store and a bakery. We got along just fine, and we're like friends."

Said Kouachi, 34 is less publicly known. His ID was discovered during the investigation of the attack, helping Police to single them out.

A U.S. official said the U.S. was given information from the French intelligence agency (DGSE) that Said Kouachi traveled to Yemen as late as 2011 on behalf of the Al Qaeda affiliate there. Once in Yemen, the older brother received a variety of weapons training from Al Qaeda in the Arabian Peninsula (AQAP) the affiliate in Yemen, including on how to fire weapons.

The two brothers were part of a network called "Buttes Chaumont", a radical young Muslims' organization. Back then, the group was part of what historian Jean-Pierre Filiu has called the third wave of "Middle Eastern–inspired terror" in France. In 2005, Benyettou and Shérif Kouachi planned to go to Iraq through Damascus, but the Police arrested them for association with a terrorist enterprise. The two men were sentenced in 2008; Shérif Kouachi, then 26, received a three-year sentence. He was released immediately, having already served that amount while awaiting trial. Benyettou admitted to having convinced people to go to Iraq and said he taught others about jihad and suicide attacks. He received a six-year sentence. It is unclear what became of Benyettou following his release and whether he and Kouachi re-linked.

Shérif Kouachi was tied to a Parisian

radical cell that has been around for a decade. Both brothers, Said and Shérif Kouachi were affiliated with al-Qaeda.

Said Kouachi received terrorist training by an Al-Qaeda affiliate in Yemen in 2011 before returning to France.

WEDNESDAY 11:20 AM

A car pulled up outside the Charlie Hebdo headquarters in Paris 11th district. Two people got out. They were dressed in black, carried what appeared to be automatic weapons and their faces covered.

The Kouachi brothers came out of the black Citroen and entered the satirical newspaper headquarters of Charlie Hebdo in Paris. One of them held an RPG missile, and both held an AK-47 Kalashnikovs rifles. Another Car was waiting for them nearby, with the driver, Hamyd Murad, an 18 years of age homeless.

Amedy Coulibaly, 32 years of age, who served time in prison for armed robbery and drug offenses with one of the Kouachi brothers, was waiting in an unknown place. Amedy Coulibaly wife, Hayat Boumeddiene, managed to flee out of the country to Turkey and from there to Syria. It was unclear whether she was at the scene at all.

"Is this the Charlie Hebdo headquarters'?" The two brothers shouted at a maintenance worker outside the office.

Some of the employees outside directed the two brothers to the magazine headquarters on the second floor, and the two moved ahead, but not before shooting to death, Eve Carson, who worked outside the headquarters of Charlie Hebdo. The Kouachi brothers entered the office. One of the employees wrote quickly on his Twitter.

"They are looking for Charlie,"

A real estate agent said that before they entered the building, the terrorists approached the person on the street and told him:

"Tell the media that al-Qaeda in Yemen."

They made their way to the magazine's headquarters on the second floor and headed to the newsroom. The two men forced Corinne Rey, an illustrator who came to work with her little daughter to enter the security code in the headquarters and allow them access to the headquarters. Corinne hides under the table with her young daughter when they came in.

"They came in and shot Boolinsky, Cabo. It lasted five minutes. I hid under the table. They spoke French perfectly; they said they were from al-Qaeda."

Florence Fovil, a sales assistant who works in the headquarters of Charlie Hebdo, testified later on:

"I saw two guns and then we heard shots. The two fires everywhere and then left the building. We were very frightened for our lives and we hid under the tables, so they won't see us. Both of them were wearing military black uniforms, from head to toe, and their faces were covered. They walk as if they were soldiers."

The staff of the magazine was in an editorial meeting when the brothers burst into the office. When they entered the office on the second floor they opened fire again. The brothers asked for specific people by name before killing them, altogether killing 10 people. The editor Hebdo and a Police Officer who was in charge of protecting him were among those killed.

Dr. Gerald Kierzek helped the wounded patients, and spoke with the survivors of the attack. He said that the brothers had divided the men from the women before opening fire.

"The shooting was not at a random spray of bullets," He said, "But more of a precision execution."

Thereafter, the brothers then left the building and drove off with a third suspect, encountering and exchanging fire with Police three times.

The only official reaction comes from a French interior minister, who said that "we are in the middle of an operation aimed to capture suspected terrorists". The Reuters' news agency reports that one person was killed in an exchange of fire.

A second Police Officer was shot and killed in the final exchange.

The armed Policeman was calling them to stop. The terrorists opened fire at him and he fell on the sidewalk. Then one of the terrorists approached him and fired at close range to confirm the killing, although the Policeman raised his hand, begging for his life.

Someone said that he heard the terrorists shouted:

"We killed Charlie Hebdo."

The terrorists have stolen a car and continued their fleeing. The Police located that getaway car in the ninth district in northern Paris, where they hijacked another car and continued running away. In the abandoned car they have found two Molotov cocktails bottles.

WEDNESDAY 11:40 AM

The terrorists themselves fled from the scene by this time conducted a large-scale hunt them all over Paris. The French government has raised the level of alert and readiness at the top level, closed the schools in the capital, and reinforced security around government buildings and other sensitive institutions. Large military forces reinforce the actions of the Police.

Lauren stranger, a writer in the office, was able to send a message to a friend.

"Call the Police. It's a massacre. It's a bloodbath. They're all dead," he said before the call was disconnected.

It appeared that the central goal of the terrorists was the editor, Stephen Sharboniih.

A Police Officer claimed that the two terrorists were looking for him inside. They were asking, 'Where are Lurking? Where is Lurking?'.

One of the journalists managed to send an SMS to a friend and said, "I am alive inside. They're all dead around me. The Jihadists sprayed me. It was definitely a massacre."

WEDNESDAY 11:50AM

The terrorists went back to the street, relaxed as they came in. Three Police Officers arrived by bicycles, but left when they saw that the terrorists were armed.

The driver of the Citroen turned back to collect the terrorists as another Police Officers arrived at the scene and start shooting at them. In response, the terrorists fired more than a dozen times.

As the three fled the scene with the Citroen they encountered another patrol car. They got out, firing in all directions, and injured a Policeman who tried to escape.

The Patrol car crashed into a parked car, and the two terrorists got out of the car and opened fire on the Police Officer from 30 feet away. He fell to the ground and held out his arms to them, pleading for his life to be spared. The two terrorists came closer and fired with their guns and shot him in the head at close range before returning to the car screaming:

"Shenkman called the Prophet Mohammed, who murdered the Charlie Hebdo."

WEDNESDAY 16:30

"The counterterrorism teams in Paris are looking for a possible hiding place the three terrorists were hiding. Few witnesses claimed that the brothers had arrived in a rented apartment in Fantine, a suburb in southeast France."

Half an hour later, thousands of people showed up in the street of Paris in favor of freedom of expression.

Police sources said that the French Police have refused to reveal the identity of the three terrorists after their Citroen car found abandoned. Later it was reported that bombs were found and flags of the Muslim' Jihadist inside.

THURSDAY 03:11

Hamyd Murad, who was waiting for two terrorists Citroen car, turned himself in to the Police. The local media reported that Murad, homeless, turned himself in after seeing his name in the social networks. It was also reported that more suspects, friends of the two Kouachi brothers were arrested.

Later on the 18-year-old Hamyd Murad stated that he was innocent. Friends of the young man state that at the time of the terrorist attack he was at school.

A statement issued by the Police, warns the public that the two brothers are "armed and dangerous," and called for the public to help locate them.

THURSDAY 08:53

As one Police Officer in Paris stopped on his way to investigate an unrelated traffic accident, he was shot with an automatic rifle by someone in a white Renault Clio car, but the shooter fled the scene.

"The Policewoman stood in front of a white car and a man fired at her and escaped," said Ahmed Sassy, a witness who lives near the site of the shooting.

"The shooter was wearing black clothes, his head was shaved, and he was wearing a bulletproof vest and carried an automatic rifle. He did not cover his face to conceal his identity. He held the gun in one hand."

THURSDAY 11:46

The French Police were concerned that the two are determined to make their way back to Paris and die in another terrorist attack. Over 100 km north-east of Paris, an owner of a gas station in Buweira-diameter Anne district, identified to the Police the two suspects in the attack.

"They wore hoods and carrying AK-47 Kalashnikovs, and rocket launchers," He said, adding that the vehicle's license plate was covered. The Police forces have surrounded the area near the gas station in Villers-Cotterets, in the northern French and set up checkpoints at 20 kilometers in all directions.

Soon after, large Police forces have located the two brothers in Anne County in the northern Picardy region. The two brothers were in a Renault Clio.

FRIDAY 01:45AM

US President Barack Obama visited the French Embassy in Washington to attend the mourning of the French people.

"As allies for centuries, we stand with our brothers in France to ensure that justice is done and that our lives will be protected," Obama wrote in the book of condolence at the scene, and signed it "Viva la France."

FRIDAY 10:28AM

Sources in the Police said that French intelligence agency (DGSE)forces, manage to pursue the two Kouachi brothers in a gun battle between the parties. The French media reported that the two brothers had kidnapped hostages and barricaded themselves in a factory near Saviour.

All roads to the village were blocked by the French intelligence forces with five helicopters circling in the air. French SWAT (National Gendarmerie Intervention Group), and the hostage rescue of France, negotiated with the terrorists. The brothers have stated to the Special Forces that are working with al-Qaeda in Yemen and told them:

"We will fight to the end."

The forces have surrounded the area near the gas station in Villers-Cotterets, in the northern French and set up checkpoints at 20 kilometers in all directions.

The French Prime Minister Manuel Valls said in an interview broadcast on local television stations in the country that his country is fighting a war on terror. French President Francois Hollande told a news conference:

"In France must provide an answer to global terrorism not only at the national level. I have confidence in our country. We have shown our ability to remain united."

FRIDAY 14:00

The shooting sounds in the Kosher Market in the 12th district of Paris. Reports in the media claimed that a terrorist barricades himself with the hostages and that he is probably responsible for the murder of Police Officer the day before.

RTL Communications reported that the brothers in eastern Paris Kosher Market demanded the release of two terrorists in the B'sharli Hebdo massacre.

Amedy Coulibaly, 32years of age, served time in prison for armed robbery and drug offenses and had contact with one of the Kouachi brothers, with him in prison.

After 3 hours and 40 minutes of drama, the Police raid Jewish supermarket in Paris and release the hostages who were held by terrorist. Four hostages were killed.

The French media reported that Police were asking journalists to stay away from the scene around the Kosher Market in Paris. It was also reported that Police ask the media to stop filming the building since the terrorist could swatch it through the media.

Amedy Coulibaly barricaded himself in the Kosher Market. Four hostages were killed by Amedy Coulibaly. Amedy Coulibaly killed them upon entering the supermarket.

FRIDAY 17:59

Explosions were also heard from the factory where the brothers were barricaded. The media reported that the two brothers were killed. The French Interior Ministry's announce.

"Our ultimate goal is to negotiate. The forces surrounding the plant want to negotiate. It can take hours or even days."

At the request of the authorities the broadcast networks stopped from broadcasting the events in the supermarket, and the journalists were removed from the site.

Shortly before 18:00 Kouachi brothers left the printing press and opened fire on the forces that surrounded the place. The Forces returned fire and killed the two. Two Officers were injured in this incident and one of them died later on.

FRIDAY 18:00

At the Jewish supermarket in Port De Experimenter in the 12th district of Paris, the forces were able to connect CCTV cameras at the market and followed Amedy. He threatened to kill hostages and demanded to allow the Kouachi brothers to leave without being harmed.

At some point he dropped to his knees to pray and the Police forces raided the place. Four hostages were killed in the terrorist attack. It turns out that the terrorist Amedy Coulibaly murdered three of them upon entering the supermarket.

Sounds of explosions and gunfire heard in place and forces went in and killed Amedy Coulibaly. They released at least five hostages, including a baby. Immediately after eliminating the terrorist Police began to search the place and found four of the hostages who were murdered in cold blood.

Some of the customers were able to escape and apparently the terrorist did not know they exist. At least one of them was able to contact a relative.

Amedy Coulibaly said he coordinated his action with the Kouachi brothers and he chose this supermarket because it was Jewish.

The operation to free the hostages at the Kosher Market began shortly after Police raided the factory where terrorists barricaded themselves.

The Le Figaro newspaper Reporter claimed that Amedy Coulibaly was with his wife, Hayat Boumeddiene, but she managed to flee out. It was unclear whether she was there at all. Later on in was confirmed that Hayat Boumedienne, fled the country 2 days before the massacre started, and flew to Turkey and from there to Syria.

FRIDAY 20:23

The French interior minister said at the scene in Paris.

"The nation felt a sigh of relief tonight." He praised the action of the security forces. "The Police allow the release of the hostages were in great danger."

French Prime Minister Manuel Valls said that the large number of the deadliest terrorist incidents in the past three days indicates the obvious failure of the security forces and intelligence officials.

A video was posted on YouTube showed the al-Qaeda leader in Yemen, saying the attack occur on the headquarters of the Charlie Hebdo was intended by the organization in response to the illustration that mocked the Prophet Mohamed.

French Interior Minister Bernard Casanova arrives at the scene of the attack and praised the actions of the security forces.

"The nation felt a sigh of relief tonight. I came here to express my thanks and gratitude to all the French people and security forces, willing to put their lives at risk."

The French interior minister told the press.

"It is difficult to protect the hostages while they in the terrorist's hands, but our forces have shown their talent and did everything to free them. We will stay on alert for the safety of all citizens."

PROLUDE

The attack in all location appeared highly organized, down to the detailed getaway plan. It's not yet clear if the brothers had additional help.

The Prime Minister claimed that the Kouachi brothers were "known to the security services." Both brothers were listed in the U.S. database of known international terrorists, known as TIDE, and had been on a no-fly list for years, a U.S. law enforcement official said.

The third suspect has turned himself in to Police. As we cleared before, Hamyd Mourad surrendered to Police late at night, after seeing his name mentioned in social media. It's also unclear what role, if any, Mourad might have had in the attack. Reports in the French media and on social platforms suggested he was at school in northeastern France at the time of the attack.

The last tweet before Wednesday's attack featured a cartoon of ISIS leader Abu Bakr Al-Baghdadi offering festive greetings with the words, "And, above all, health!"

THE VICTIMS

At least 12 people were killed in the attack, including Police Officers and cartoonists. Charlie Hebdo the editor and Stephane Charbonnier were among the dead.

Seven journalists were killed, including well-known cartoonists Georges Wolinski, who worked under the pen name Wolinski, Jean Cabot, Bernard Verlhac and Philippe Honore.

The economist and a Charlie Hebdo shareholder, Bernard Maris, were also reported killed.

According to authorities a maintenance man and two Police Officers also died.

The two Police Officers killed were identified as Ahmed Merabet and Franck Brinsolaro.

In the attack, eleven other people were wounded, including four in serious condition.

All the victims have been identified, but over time, more stories of these lives cut so tragically short by terrorism is likely to emerge.

The Eiffel Tower was darkened in memory of the victims.

IN THE AFTERMATH

The FBI and U.S. intelligence agencies are mapping the suspects' relationships for clues, including digital records. They were running the Kouachi brothers names through databases and looked for connections with ISIS and Al Qaeda.

The Investigators are also trying to establish whether this was a one-off attack or part of a bigger coordinated strategy.

France still found it difficult to read the writing on the wall. The French President Francois Hollande, who visited the newspaper headquarters the terrorist attacks, was refrained from pointing a direct finger at the ideology behind the act.

The massacre in the Charlie Hebdo headquarters can be explained as an act of individuals, but it's clear that this only a symptom of the problem rooted much deeper, and is a more serious disease, which threatens France, and whole Europe, it's the radical Islam disease. Come to think of it, a whopping fifth of the members of the Muslim community, living in France, have sympathy to the ISIS organization. This is the breeding grounds for radical Islamic terrorism in France.

France has already voiced and expresses an understanding even though they strongly condemn the terrorist attack. After all the Charlie Hebdo newspaper published a few weeks ago, a cartoon depicting heads back on Jihadist slit the throat of the Prophet Muhammad. At that time, witnesses testified that they heard terrorists will take revenge.

But the French must realize that when they fighting against terrorism, there should be no discounts. With all due respect, understanding the motives of the killers should last on the list and regardless, they must be separated from fighting them to the death.

The attack shows that we can no longer disconnect between what is happening in the Middle East and what happens in Europe. The Mass migration of millions of Muslims to Western Europe and the formation of large Muslim communities, which are unable or refuse to assimilate with the western culture, created a situation in which ISIS is feeling at home there, nesting among young Muslims who are misled and want to fight for something never existed.

France is participating in the campaign against ISIS and is working against radical Islam in Africa. Moreover, the leader of ISIS, Caliph Abu Bakr Al-Baghdadi, announced that its goal is "liberate Europe" in the name of Islam, and therefore if anyone in Europe is asked to disengage from any involvement in the Middle East they be going to find out that the Middle East will chase after them.

Stephane Charbonnier, the illustrator and editor of the newspaper, who was murdered in the terrorist attack two years ago, said to the newspaper Le Monde.

"I rather die standing than live on my knees."

Based on the evidence gathered so far, it is apparent that this massacre was planned and targeted in advance. The attack was based on prior intelligence information. The British newspaper "Daily Telegraph" published that some of the witnesses who were at the scene claimed that prior to the massacre the terrorists shouted that they belong to the Yemeni branch of the "al-Qaeda".

Upon entering the place, the terrorists called the names of the seniors including the chief editor and cartoonist Stephane

Charbonnier and his colleagues. Also called the names of cartoonists Jean Cabo, and Georges Wolinski, the 80-year-old Jewish. He was a Holocaust survivor.

France is a nation that is considered the homeland of democracy and its motto, Liberté, Égalité, Fraternité (**Liberty, Equality, and Fraternity**) speak for itself.

The Islamic terrorism, hitting Paris on January 7, punched a hole in the symbol of liberty and the freedom of expression human rights. The war reaches their door. The event shocked not only France, but the entire West. The question was not if, the question was when and where. You can call it Jihad.

The scary images that are usually seen in Syria and Iraq are now taking place and sponsored by the Jihad and the Islamic terrorism in one of the most beautiful cities we love to love.

The Jihad gave himself a "license to kill" in the heart of the West. Passport control, by the way, is not relevant anymore. As a Trojan horse, Jihad has been already penetrating deep inside Paris, Brussels, Madrid and London.

We live in an age of political correctness that condemns anyone who dares to call a spade a spade. It's a common thread in all the attacks, and it's the radical Islam.

Any 'Charlie Hebdo' who dared to mock Islam and the Prophet just as it did for all religions will find himself in the danger zone. Four incidents occurred in France before Christmas, and the Republic came to realized that this was not just a craze and more classic terrorist attack.

For a change Francois Hollande rushed to call as the French say: 'call a cat a cat.'

The question is what's next. Assuming that tomorrow will be easier for France to fight radical Islam in Iraq, Afghanistan, Syria, but continues to avoid the inevitable war against terrorism in the name of European humanism, which prefers to explain the radical Islam as a socioeconomic problem and not an asymmetric war.

Even President Obama and European leaders asked to delete the term radical Islam, in order not to hurt the Muslim population. In order not to frighten the western population, not to anger the migrants to the West in general and to look the other direction, particularly in France.

Circles in the intelligence and combat terrorism in Europeans countries have raised, a serious concerns that the terrorist attacks in the center of Paris, is only the first in a series of terrorist attacks to be happening soon in France, and possibly also in other European capitals. France raised the alert level to the terrorist attacks to the highest level. In London, Berlin, Madrid, Hague and Rome, and the major airports in Europe, the alert level was also raised among the security forces.

The action and behavior of the attackers, shows a higher level of training of their assassins, and it's indicative to fighters of Al Qaeda or ISIS, who acquired combat experience in the battlefield of Syria and Iraq.

In 2011 Charlie Hebdo published cartoons satirizing Mohammed. The satirical newspaper published a New Year's Eve greeting card ridiculed Al-Qaeda's head of ISIS, Abu Bakr Al-Baghdadi.

The spokesman to the French intelligence agency (DGSE) said that his view is strengthened after it became clear that the two assassins dressed in black uniforms with black masks on their faces, we're holding lists of journalists, and asking the names of everyone they met in the corridors. When they discovered that it was a listed journalist they shot him. He added that the level of armaments, their shooting precision, especially with the French Police, and their escape route from the scene, shows that they are professional assassins operating in cold blood.

It is now clear that the intelligence services in French, who were already on high alert after several shooting incidents on Jewish targets in Paris, were doomed to fail.

The reason is that. There are about six million Muslims in France, and they constitute much more than 10% of its population. Among the EU countries, France is the second after Bulgaria in the percentage of the Muslim population in the total population. The AK-47 Kalashnikov is a Russian assault rifle and the standard weapon in the Islamist organizations. They were trained in their use it and harm many people in minimal time and escape with a prepared planned in advance. It is a small weapon and very easy to use. Plus, many of the eastern European countries has those rifles in the black market selling for 2000- $3000 dollar.

We are now facing a global phenomenon of individuals who attacks, carrying suicide bombs, and it's now spreads across the entire globe. But now it's clear what the definition of mental disorder or criminal background is. Its features an easy diagnosis: cold weapons (knives, axes), rage and, less often, firearms coming from the criminal world. The terrorists themselves operate for three main reasons:

Usually it's the individual in a process of becoming Islamist, but the religious element is dominant. Most of them suffer from mental disorder or mental illness of the some sort. Typically, those individual terrorists are not mentally ill, such as justifying a prolonged hospitalization. You know the rest.

The tricky part is that these few individuals are too difficult to detect in advance. Just because he was praying to

Mecca five times a day and suffer from a mental disorder doesn't mean there is a justification for terrorizing the world.

The first picture published in a magazine in Paris after the massacre shows pages stained with blood all over the hallway, chilling evidence of the terrorist attack in Charlie Hebdo headquarters.

So far there was only a delegation of 20 Muslim imams who condemned the massacre.

"They are criminals, barbarians, devils. For me they are not Muslims," said the Imam of Paris.

"Their hatred, their barbarism, has nothing to do with Islam. We are all French, we are all human. We have to live with dignity, tolerance and solidarity."

As a revenge for the massacre some anonymous people had thrown three grenades into a mosque in La Mans, France. In southern France the prayer' room was empty, and the walls of the mosque was sprayed "Death to Arabs".

In Eastern France, near the town of Lyon, an explosion occurred outside the kebab stand near a mosque. No one was injured.

"Muslims in France have a feeling that they are second-class citizens," said Bubakor, a senior in the Great Mosque in Paris.

Rashid Abdul Rahim, 22-year-old student, lives in Paris. He said that when he heard that the three terrorists are Muslims is quickly said.

"We are going to be bad from now on. Before we were shooting an ordinary person who does not like Muslims, but now we will do much worse." Samir said, "When some people see terrorists, they are confusing them with other Muslims. The next victim will be a Muslim for sure."

According to a recent survey published in Paris, 72% of the French people see the Muslims in a flattering way, compared to 28% in Italy and 58% in Germany.

Some of the most severe reactions to the terrorism in Paris came from Germany. The National Democratic NPD, called its supporters to demonstrate against the Islamic community. "If it happened in Paris it can happen also in Berlin."

"Muslim leaders apologize now but the French still close their eyes."

One thing for sure. When Muslims start to be afraid and everything will calm and we will have peace! Look at those figures:

The population of Muslim in the world is 23 % or 1.9 billion Muslims. 20% of those are radical Muslims which is 400.000.000 suicidal people in the world. Why is it that the remaining 80% of Muslims who consider themselves normal, are not speaking? They are afraid that the truth about their true intentions is revealed. It's true that not all Muslims are terrorists, but what can you do that all terrorists are Muslims? The Europeans finally understand who they were dealing with. As it say in the Arab world:

"If you sleep with dogs don't be surprised if you wake up with mites..."

WHAT'S NEXT?

According to the 'Le Monde' newspaper, Amedy Coulibaly and Shérif Kouachi have religiously followed Jamal Bghal, a French-Algerian who was convicted of intent to attack the American embassy in France. He was arrested in 2001 in the UAE and sentenced in 2005 to 10 years in prison but was released three years ago. Those phone calls show that Amedy Coulibaly and Shérif Kouachi have visited Bengals' home who was continually claiming that he had met with Osama bin Laden in the past.

The French Police are also looking for Hayat Boumeddiene, a young woman of 26, who was the partner of Amedy Coulibaly since 2010. It remains unclear whether she was with her boyfriend/husband in the supermarket.

Amedy Coulibaly has a criminal past served a prison sentence. It was a minor in respect of the armed robbery and the drug offenses. The Relationship between Amedy Coulibaly and Kouachi tightened up while they both were serving prison in Floari Mrg'oai jail, in south of Paris, where Amedy Coulibaly had converted to Islam.

Amedy Coulibaly was arrested again in 2010 on a suspicion of being behind an attempt to help Jasmine Eagle, who was responsible for the attack on a train in Paris in 1995. In the search of his house, four years ago the Police found much ammunition for AK-47 Kalashnikov rifles. He was sent to prison and released over in 2013. According to one account, Amedy Coulibaly and the two Kouachi brothers belong to the same group of Jihad. Amedy Coulibaly is also shot him the Police Officer with an automatic rifle and murdered him while the officer was on his way to investigate a car accident.

A witness told the Police that the gunman was wearing black clothing and a bulletproof vest, his head was shaved and he did not cover his face in an attempt to hide his identity. Amedy wore the exact same clothes the next day in the Kosher Market.

At the same time, the brothers Said, and Shérif, already besieged by the Police who surround them and declared:

"We want to die as martyrs." They barricaded themselves in a pattern while holding at least one of the hostages.

Meanwhile in Paris, in the Kosher Market Amedy Coulibaly continue to barricade himself with hostages, as the Police ordered all the shops in that area to close their doors, and all Jews in that area were barred from attending the near synagogue. Police continue to besiege the kosher supermarket.

Earlier that day French Police said that the kidnappers are the same terrorist who killed yesterday Police woman Bmonrose, in the south of the city, and they are trying to locate two suspects: Amedy Coulibaly, and Hayat Boumedienne. Soon after, Amedy Coulibaly demanded to free the two brothers. "Le Figaro" claimed that the brothers and threatened to kill hostages.

As the two brothers reached near the village the Police asked residents to stay home, and students in three schools in the area were ordered not to leave their classrooms and stay away from the windows.

"Some of the students were crying, scared to death, and some were understating the incident," one of the students told "Le

Figaro."

Another student said: "It is total terrorism. Shooting at my school! We are locked in our class and are not allowed outside."

"Everyone was stuck in their homes behind locked doors," someone who lived just 300 meters from the printing factory said as he realized that something was wrong. He was happy to see the large Police force comes to the area with helicopters in the air. The SWAT team from the counterterrorism units acted competently, systematically and diligently. They have collected most of the needed intelligence by using a closed circuit camera. They also placed explosives near the doors in both places, to break-in quickly.

When Saíd and Shérif Kouachi barricaded themselves in a pattern they did not see Lillian, 27 years old was hiding in a small cardboard box at the factory. From his hiding place he reported to the security forces every movement of the terrorists and the exact layout of the building. Lillian works as a graphic designer in this printing house, with his father running the two-story factory. His father, Pascal was also at the factory when the terrorists arrived. Witnesses said that about three hours after their fortifications Pascal managed to escape and reached the Police forces. Lillian remained in hiding for more than six hours and passed critical information about the Kouachi brothers.

Shortly after the takeover of the factory Lillian sent a message to his father, Pascal which indicates that he didn't know the whereabouts of his son when he escaped from his workplace.

Lillian continued to provide vital information to the Police over the phone while snipers took positions on nearby rooftops and helicopters arrived at the scene. Paris prosecutor Francois Moulin said that he was scared, but managed to convey tactical information.

The SWAT Police made a decision to open fire when Shérif and Said Kouachi began praying. An explosion heard and within a minute the two were eliminated. The big explosion appears to be from the printing factory where the two brothers were hiding. Shérif and Said Kouachi opened fire on the troops who surrounded the place. The Police SWAT team returned fire, killed them both, and rescued the hostage.

Lillian came out of his hiding, was taken for psychological assessment, and then he returns to his family.

So, a few minutes a fter the operation started at the printing factory, a secondary force broke into the Jewish Market. The French Interior Ministry issued a misleading message that he intends to negotiate with the terrorists.

Ingenuity, skill and practice paid off early. But unfortunately most of the victims were killed by the terrorist prior to the Police break-in. The French Interior Ministry perhaps should be proud that both operations conducted in this parallel rescue.

It was said before that Said Kouachi was trained in Yemen and al-Qaeda was positions there. His older brother Shérif was convicted and jailed when Muslims recruited to fight in the ranks of al-Qaeda in Syria and he tried to go there himself. Both were removed from the watch list of the French intelligence services in last two years. Why? The French intelligence forces had a limited means in controlling the enormous population of potential Muslim terrorists.

The French intelligence agency has conducted an extensive manhunt throughout France, for Hayat Boumediene, after she managed to escape from Paris.

Hayat Boumeddiene married Amedy Coulibaly in 2009, and never left him. She declared openly, even to investigators summoned her from time to time, 'that she is dedicated to Coulibaly', and she devoted herself to him. There is a real concern among French intelligence agency is that Hayat will try to avenge the death of her husband, and the death of Said and Shérif Kouachi.

The French intelligence agency is not alone or orphaned for this problem. It's shared by most of the Western intelligence agencies, including the FBI, and the British MI5 and MI6.

The threat of a mass casualty attack is a growing concern among all the intelligence communities and their ability of pointing out the existence of specific plots may be untimely. The question is not the level of threats, but how to prevent them, and there is no answer to this question in the intelligence agencies.

The French intelligence agency, the DGSE has tremendous budgets and technology, and their failure to find the Kouachi brothers, not just before the attack in Paris, but also after it, is a symptom of most intelligence communities blindness, which caused by sole dependency on technology. The extreme shortage of tactical intelligence information, about terrorist and their organizations as well as the lack of understanding of their attitudes and trends among millions of Muslims in major Western cities is the resulting factor in the tragic massacre in Charlie Hebdo headquarters.

This Jihadi, Amedy Coulibaly had murdered a woman Police Officer in Paris and was heard having a bizarre conversation with one of the hostages before he was shot dead by the French forces. At the time he was holding at least a dozen people hostage.

When the phone line in the Market rang, Amedy Coulibaly was overheard, blaming the French military action in Mali, Syria and the Islamic State for his own bloody supermarket siege.

But Coulibaly left the line open for several minutes while it captured Amedy Coulibaly speaking to a hostage.

During a five-minute ranting, Coulibaly was heard saying: "Every time, they try to make you think that Muslims are terrorists. I was born in France. If they hadn't been attacking everywhere, I wouldn't be here."

And later on Coulibaly added:

"I'll tell them to stop attacking the Islamic State, and stop unveiling our women, and stop putting our brothers in prison for everything and anything."

One of the hostages talk with a broken voice to say that he is not responsible for the actions of their government, but Coulibaly answered:

"You're the one who elected your governments, and the governments never hide their intentions to be at war in Mali or elsewhere."

For a minute, it was understood from the conversation that Coulibaly has claimed at one point that he would kill his hostages if the French Police tried to move-in.

At 3pm the TV station received a call from Amedy Coulibaly and he spoke with the journalist.

Journalist: "Are you linked with the two brothers who did the shooting at Charlie Hebdo?"

Amedy: "We synchronized to do the operations."

Journalist: "Are you still in contact with them? Have you spoken on the phone with them?"

Amedy: "No"

Journalist: "How did you synchronize? Do you have other events planned? Do you have a scenario that you are following?"

Amedy: "No, we just decided at the

start, so they did Charlie Hebdo and I took care of Police Officers."

* * * * *

At the printing factory Shérif Kouachi was speaking to a journalist who recorded the conversation as it was:

Shérif Kouachi: "We are just telling you that we are the defenders of the prophet (Muhammad), and that I Shérif Kouachi has been sent by Al Qaida of Yemen, and I went over there and that Anwar Al Awaki has financed me."

Journalist: "And approximately how long ago was that?"

Kouachi: "E..... It was a while ago before he was killed."

* * * * *

Asana levies was born as a Muslim in Mali and immigrated to France. He worked at the kosher market on Friday when Amedy Coulibaly launched the attack on the market and took hostages. Asana shoved 6 of his customers into the freezer and asked them to stay quiet. Among the people was a month old baby. Saved the lives of six Jews.

Asana recalled the dramatic moments:

"They wanted to go down. I opened the freezer door, and I went along with them. Then, he turned off the light and the freezer's cooling system. I went out of the cooler and told them to remain calm."

Other customers of the kosher market were hiding in the supermarket talked about the horror's hours to the media: one man named Michel said.

"I stood in front of the cashier to pay and I heard a loud noise, such as distillation. I wasn't worried until I saw a black man, armed, and immediately I understood what was happening, I took my son by the neck and pulled him to the end of the store. Along with several customers, we went down, and we went into one of the big refrigerator rooms. And we were very afraid. The terrorist searched for us but the door was locked from the inside, and he couldn't open it. Later on he screamed to tell us that if we don't go out there will be a massacre."

Michelle initially refused the request.

"We heard the terrorist turned the shelves upside down with his weapons and said that death is a reward for him. After a while he began to pray and the Police have heard it all. There was a terrible noise and multiple shooting. A few seconds later, we opened the door, and we realized it was the end. So we went outside."

* * * * *

Despite last Islamic massacre occurred in Paris, it seems that nothing has really changed in the thinking of the French government, the extreme political liberalism; the European leaders refrained from declaring the fight against Islamic terrorism. The French Prime Minister, Manuel Valls, said, "We do not conduct a war against religion, but against the Terrorism."

That's the main problem of in Europe. How can you win if you cannot define who is your enemies? The Islamic radicals continue to benefit from the soft hand, which allow them to raise their head again and again.

There is no shame in defining the enemy, to be realistic, and to recognize the facts. France is a country of all its citizens, in which religion and origin do not play any role.

This is the root of Europe defeat before they fell at the feet of spreading Islam:

The Western democracies ready to believe that if we do one more tribute, it will buy a few years of quiet and peace. The French Police claimed that Boumeddiene, the wife of the Amedy Coulibaly, participated on Friday of terrorist acts in the Kosher Market in Paris, and managed to escape with the Jewish hostages and then disappeared, while actually all this time she was in Syria.

All they had to do is check the listings in the border security system in France, Spain and Turkey, to find that Hayat Boumeddiene left France on January second, two days before the attack on Charlie Hebdo headquarters. That means that she could not have been involved in the attack on Friday in the kosher market in Paris. While the Police fed this imaginary details to the French media, they themselves operated by an assumption that do not exist in reality. This by itself completely blurs the picture further if someone wants to determine who was really behind the attacks in Paris. One more thing. Some government sources have made a great effort to point the responsibility to Al Qaeda in Yemen, AQAP. The reason appeared to be clear: to keep for later the possibility that Al Qaeda in Iraq and the ISIS, is the one behind the attacks in France.

And if Hayat Boumeddiene flew from France to Syria, a day or two before the wave of attacks started it might be that she was the force behind it all and went to the same place where she can manage the operation in Paris.

FINAL WORDS

Despite the rain and cold, millions streamed from early morning to walk in Republic Square. At least three million and 700 thousand people demonstrated Across France in memory of the victims of the terror attacks in Paris. They came with flags, with parents, with children and with pencils, in memory of members of the Charlie Hebdo. It was the largest show of unity the country's history.

The rally in Paris attended by more than a million and a half people, and over a million demonstrated in other cities in France.

Thirty-eight heads of state marched in central Paris and stood in silence in memory of the 17 people murdered by the terrorist. The families of the murdered in the attack wore white ribbons on their heads and saying "Charlie". The French President Francois Hollande came to shake their hands. Four families of Jewish victims, cap on their heads, looked painful, sad as any of the Jewish community in France.

Many participants carried signs with the name of the magazine. Other rallies of solidarity were held around the world, including Germany, United Kingdom, Belgium, Italy, Canada, and Austria. In many other cities, people came to say: "Enough terrorism. Enough hatred. Enough to be afraid."

It is unclear what the future holds. Paris returned to normal and the Metro station in East Jerusalem has been reopened. The demonstration ended at the Place De La Nation.

It remains to be seen what the government will do with the great credit given to them. The victims were killed while exercising their most basic rights of freedom of expression.

The enemy of all is the radical Islam and the Islamic extremism. The Radical Islam hates the West. Those who massacred the Jews and the journalists in Paris belong to the same murderous terrorist movement, and we should have the power to fight them.

In response to the demonstration of the millions against terrorism in France, the senior leader of ISIS announced that his commanders pledge their loyalty and commitment to Abu Bakr Al-Baghdadi Al-

Qaeda. Immediately after the announcement they beheaded a Pakistani soldier who was held captive by them.

Radical Islamic preacher from London informed that insulting the Prophet Muhammad marks the end of Arab civilization, and the future of the Islamic takeover of the world.

"Muslim who is willing accept the insulting the prophet, are not Muslim." He threatened, "If Charles Hebdo will publish other cartoons, and there will be revenge."

It is very clear that Muslims are willing to give their self-esteem and dignity for the Prophet.

However, this preacher in London turns around and refused to take responsibility for terrorist acts around the world and just said that it's impossible to stop people who take the law into their own hands if there is another provocation against the Muslim community in Europe. However, he could not explain the reason that in the Muslim world there were not many condemnations against the massacre.

"Allah will send his punishment, which signs the end of Western civilization and the spread of Islam throughout the world." He said.

The End